MW01130622

Millie Finds
Her Miracle

Courtney Mount

Illustrations by Amber Andersen

Millie Finds Her Miracle

Text © 2022 by Courtney Mount
Illustrations © 2022 by Amber Andersen
Print ISBN: 978-1-66787-963-5
Printed in the United States of America.

Acknowledgements:

**To all the parents who have ever had to walk a child to heaven,
my heart is with you.**

**To Amber Andersen who took my idea and my heart thoughts,
then drew them for the world to see.**

To Millie's Miracle readers who encouraged and faithfully prayed for me.

**To Millie for the many things that she taught me in her three years:
her courage, strength, faith, and especially unconditional love.**

To my other children who have given me time to tell this story.

To Millie's Daddy who walked every step of this journey with me.

**To God who has sustained me in my sorrow, put joy in my heart,
and given me that peace that passes understanding in the face of pain.**

Hi, I'm Millie and this is the story
of me and my miracle.

As I search for my miracle, can you find
the butterfly on each page?

A miracle can look
like so many things:

colorful rainbows in the sky,
a newborn baby,
a beautiful butterfly,
or the way God can heal our
bodies when we are sick.

Long before I arrived, Mama and Daddy were watching for their newest miracle.

They looked high,
and they looked low,

but they did not know just how close
their miracle was until one day...

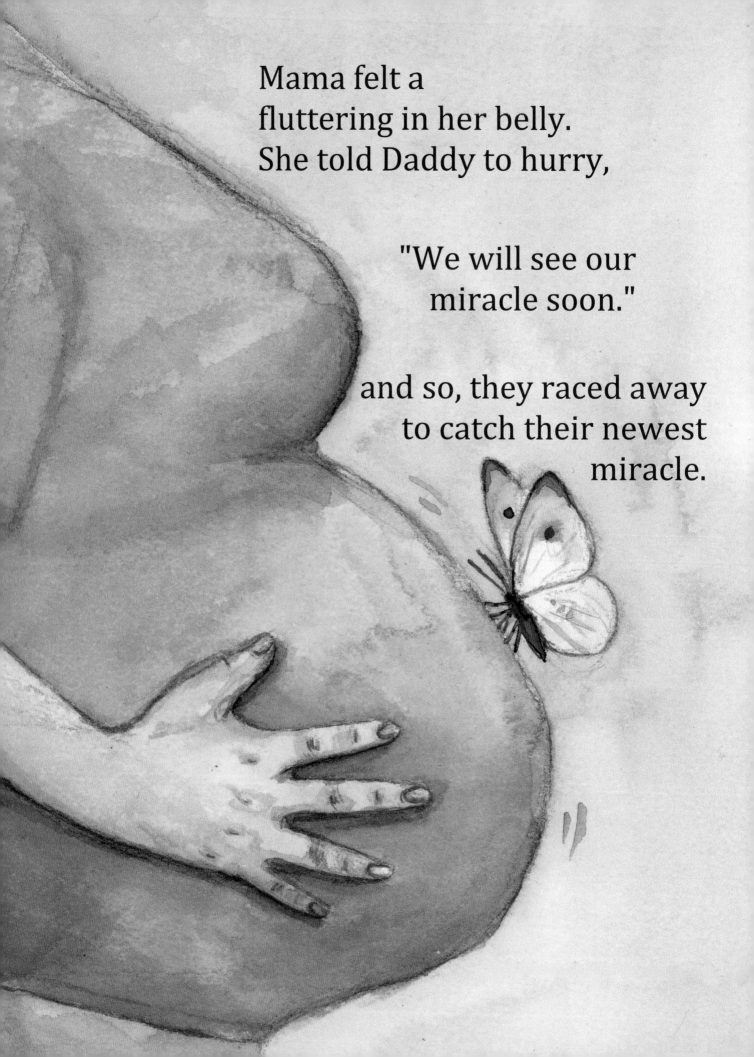

Mama felt a
fluttering in her belly.
She told Daddy to hurry,

"We will see our
miracle soon."

and so, they raced away
to catch their newest
miracle.

The moment I was born, Mama and Daddy knew their miracle had entered the room.

"Millie is beautiful!" said Daddy.

"What a precious baby!" cooed Mama.

"It is a miracle you made it to the hospital!" said the doctor.

All around me I saw different kinds of
miracles. Some miracles were big,
and some were very tiny.
A few of them were colorful and bright.

I knew I wanted to find
a miracle of my very own
but which one would be mine?

While playing in the evening light,
I spotted beautiful sparkly
diamonds twinkling all
around me.

Maybe my miracle
could look like that?

As Daddy and I took walks on our farm,
I searched for my miracle.

I spotted a newborn calf
resting in the hay.

Furry kittens were
chasing and frolicking in
the sunshine.

I even petted our llama named Hope.
I just couldn't catch sight of my miracle!

One summer day my
tummy started to hurt,
and I got really sick.
"Owie!" I cried.

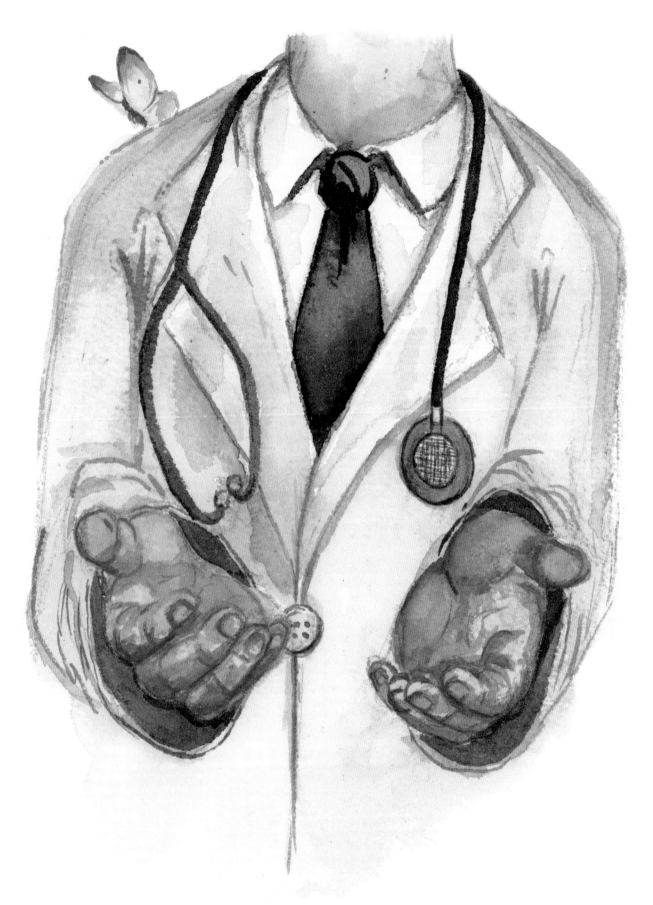

Mama and Daddy took me to the hospital.
The doctor said, "Millie needs a miracle!"

Mama and Daddy started
searching everywhere to
help me find my miracle.

The doctors joined in the search too!

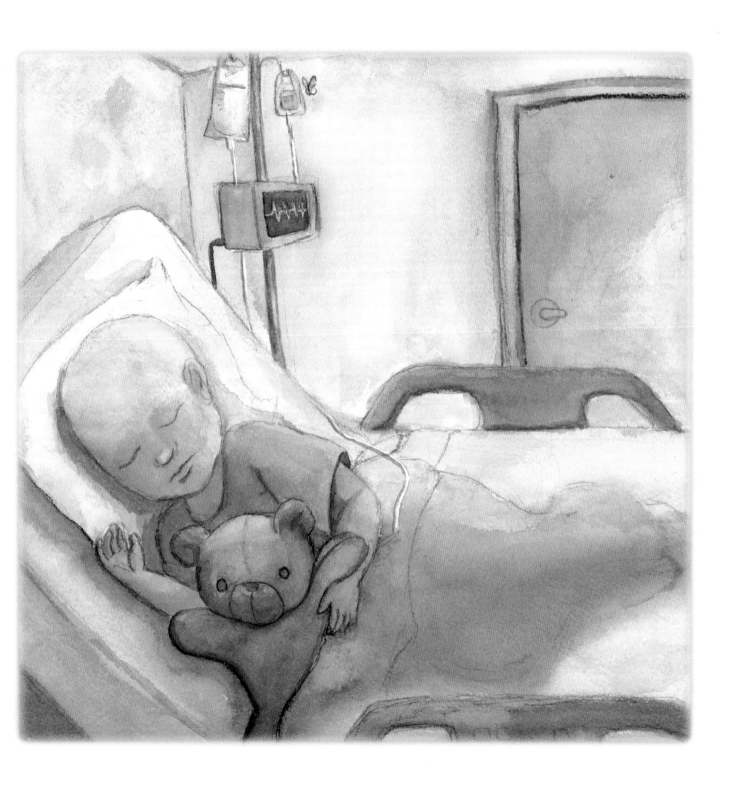

I had to stay in the hospital for a long time
while everyone searched for my miracle.

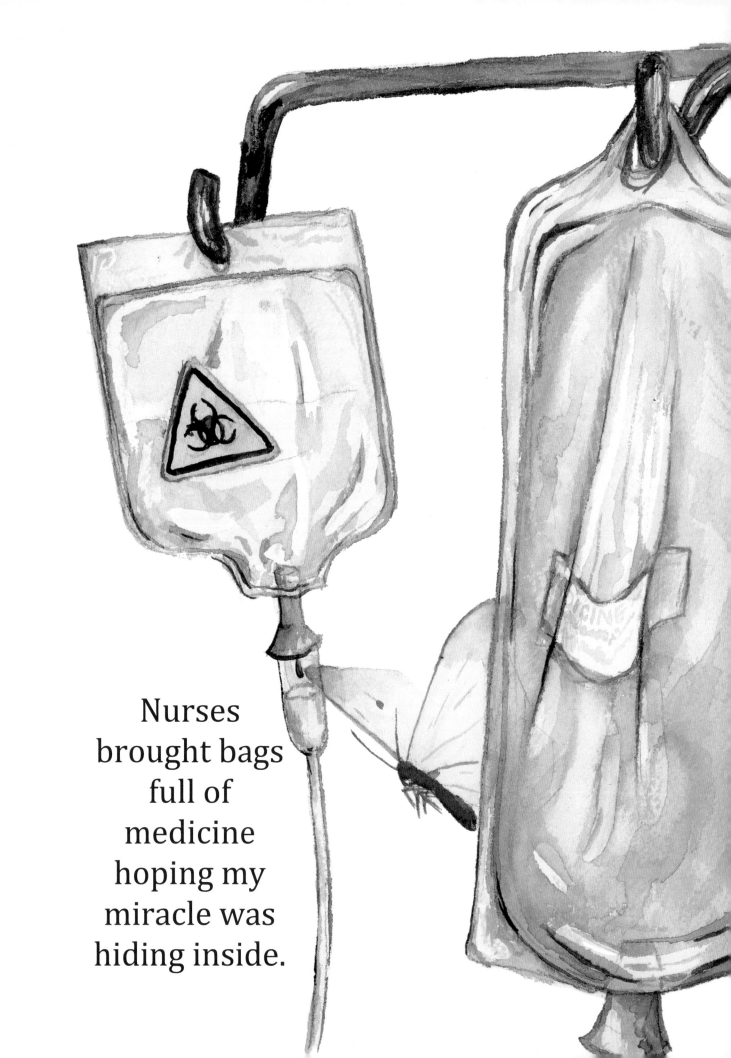

Nurses
brought bags
full of
medicine
hoping my
miracle was
hiding inside.

I had to go visit special machines that looked inside my body to see if my miracle had come to take my sickness away.

When I got to go back home, I searched
in my playground, always watching
for my beautiful miracle to appear.

"Oh Miracle... Where are YOU?" I loudly called out.

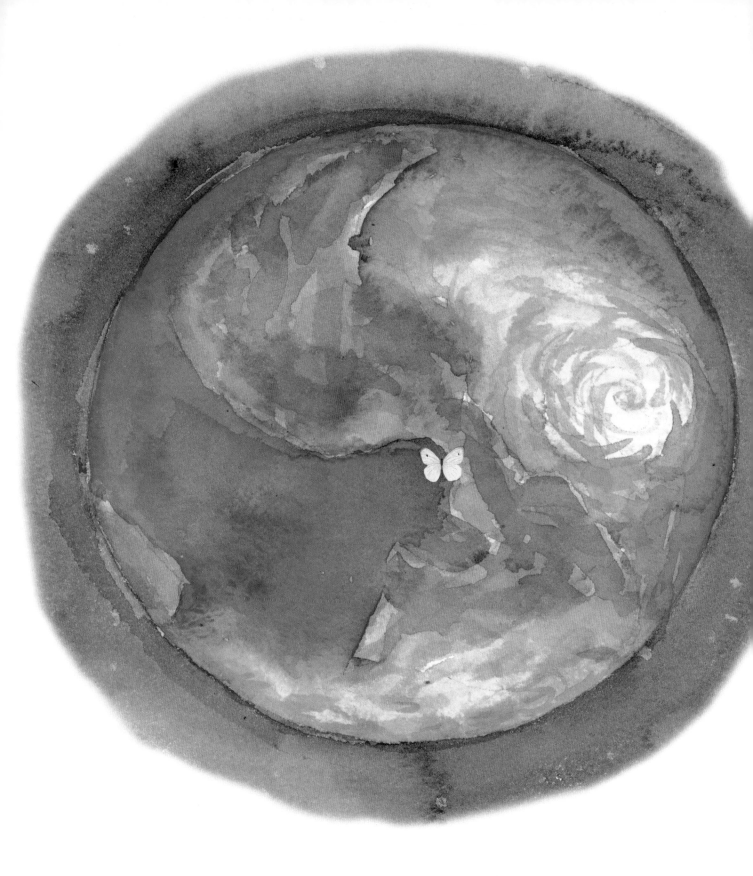

Every day, people around the world
prayed for my miracle to come
close enough for me to catch it.

My family prayed too, "Lord Jesus, please give Millie her miracle." They knew when I found my miracle I wouldn't feel sick or have owies anymore.

One day, I heard a soft whisper,
"Millie, come into my garden.
I have your Miracle ready."

I finally found my beautiful Miracle

in Heaven with Jesus.

All about me...

Amelia Joy Mount, fondly called Millie, was diagnosed at the age of two and a half years old with stage 4 Neuroblastoma, an aggressive childhood cancer. She fought for her earthly life for over a year and on July 8, 2020, she found her miracle of healing as she entered into eternal life with Jesus.

A note from Mama and Daddy:

On each page of Millie Finds Her Miracle, butterflies were used to represent a miracle. Millie's diagnosis was similar to an ugly caterpillar who goes though the hardest things in life. The caterpillar has a horrible change ahead of him. Entering into his chrysalis, he waits with no hope, but then a miracle transforms him into a beautiful butterfly.

While a terminal diagnosis is a devastating thing to hear, you are not alone. God can use your story and turn it into one of beauty. The Bible tells us that there is no more pain or sadness for those in heaven. However, we know that for those of us left behind, the pain of child loss is still very evident. Our hope lies in knowing Jesus as our Lord and Savior. His promise of a life in heaven means we also have hope of seeing our precious children again one day.

Millie's Miracle

Now faith is confidence in what we hope for and assurance about what we do not see.
Hebrews 11:1